TRENDS IN SOUTHEAST ASIA

The **ISEAS – Yusof Ishak Institute** (formerly Institute of Southeast Asian Studies) is an autonomous organization established in 1968. It is a regional centre dedicated to the study of socio-political, security, and economic trends and developments in Southeast Asia and its wider geostrategic and economic environment. The Institute's research programmes are grouped under Regional Economic Studies (RES), Regional Strategic and Political Studies (RSPS), and Regional Social and Cultural Studies (RSCS). The Institute is also home to the ASEAN Studies Centre (ASC), the Temasek History Research Centre (THRC) and the Singapore APEC Study Centre.

ISEAS Publishing, an established academic press, has issued more than 2,000 books and journals. It is the largest scholarly publisher of research about Southeast Asia from within the region. ISEAS Publishing works with many other academic and trade publishers and distributors to disseminate important research and analyses from and about Southeast Asia to the rest of the world.

FROM *TAO GUANG YANG HUI* TO *XIN XING*

China's Complex Foreign Policy Transformation and Southeast Asia

Pang Zhongying

ISSUE

7

2020

YUSOF ISHAK
INSTITUTE

Published by: ISEAS Publishing
                  30 Heng Mui Keng Terrace
                  Singapore 119614
                  publish@iseas.edu.sg
                  http://bookshop.iseas.edu.sg

ISEAS Library Cataloguing-in-Publication Data

Name(s): Pang, Zhongying, 1962–
Title: From *Tao Guang Yang Hui* to *Xin Xing* : China's Complex Foreign Policy Transformation and Southeast Asia / Pang Zhongying.
Description: Singapore : ISEAS – Yusof Ishak Institute, June 2020. | Series: Trends in Southeast Asia, ISSN 0219-3213 ; TRS7/20 | Includes bibliographical references.
Identifiers: ISBN 9789814881807 (paperback) | ISBN 9789814881814 (PDF)
Subjects: LCSH: China—Foreign relations—20th century. | China—Foreign relations—21st century.
Classification: LCC DS501 I59T no. 7(2020)

Typeset by Superskill Graphics Pte Ltd
Printed in Singapore by Markono Print Media Pte Ltd

FOREWORD

The economic, political, strategic and cultural dynamism in Southeast Asia has gained added relevance in recent years with the spectacular rise of giant economies in East and South Asia. This has drawn greater attention to the region and to the enhanced role it now plays in international relations and global economics.

The sustained effort made by Southeast Asian nations since 1967 towards a peaceful and gradual integration of their economies has had indubitable success, and perhaps as a consequence of this, most of these countries are undergoing deep political and social changes domestically and are constructing innovative solutions to meet new international challenges. Big Power tensions continue to be played out in the neighbourhood despite the tradition of neutrality exercised by the Association of Southeast Asian Nations (ASEAN).

The **Trends in Southeast Asia** series acts as a platform for serious analyses by selected authors who are experts in their fields. It is aimed at encouraging policymakers and scholars to contemplate the diversity and dynamism of this exciting region.

THE EDITORS

Series Chairman:
   Choi Shing Kwok

Series Editor:
   Ooi Kee Beng

Editorial Committee:
   Daljit Singh
   Francis E. Hutchinson
   Benjamin Loh

From *Tao Guang Yang Hui* to *Xin Xing*: China's Complex Foreign Policy Transformation and Southeast Asia

Pang Zhongying

EXECUTIVE SUMMARY

- This article traces China's foreign policy transformation from 2013 to the present. It also examines Deng Xiaoping's doctrinal response to the political crises of 1989–91 and compares it to current Chinese foreign policy doctrines.
- From the early 1980s until the 2010s, China's foreign policy has generally focused on keeping a low profile. Deng's *Tao Guang Yang Hui* foreign policy doctrine is characterized by its "No's", while Xi Jinping's *Xin Xing* is marked by its "New's". The move from *Tao Guang Yang Hui* to *Xin Xing* is a major doctrinal shift in China's foreign policy.
- Since the 19th Party Congress in 2017, Xi's "new" narratives have seemingly dominated Chinese foreign policy. However, old principles, particularly that of "non-interference" or "no hegemony", are still alive, albeit in a different form.
- This transformation is driven by three forces, which this paper describes in the 3As framework: China's *Ambition* to be a "great country" and a "non-hegemon" in a changing world; its provision of *Alternatives* to fill the gaps in regional and global governance structures; and its *Adaptation* to what it deems as "unprecedented major changes in a century" (*Da Bian Ju*).
- As China undergoes this foreign policy transformation, contradictions and dilemmas inevitably emerge.
- While China's foreign policy transformation is currently being disrupted by the coronavirus crisis, there have been adjustments

which were already apparent before the crisis. The ambitious "One Belt and One Road" strategy, for instance, was replaced by the "Belt and Road Initiative"; "constructive intervention" was replaced by "constructive role"; and "common destiny" was replaced by "shared future". Looking ahead, China's foreign policy transformation could include more strategic or, at least, tactical adjustments.

From *Tao Guang Yang Hui* to *Xin Xing*: China's Complex Foreign Policy Transformation and Southeast Asia

Pang Zhongying[1]

As Singapore clocked its first handful of coronavirus cases in late January 2020, Singapore Prime Minister Lee Hsien Loong, while on the sidelines of the World Economic Forum in Switzerland, issued an appeal for the public to remain calm.[2] This appeal bore some similarities with China's former paramount leader Deng Xiaoping's *Tao Guang Yang Hui* (韬光养晦) foreign policy doctrine—to calmly observe, hold one's ground, react firmly, act but keep a low profile (冷静观察、稳住阵脚、沉着应付、韬光养晦、有所作为: *leng jing guan cha, wen zhu zhen jiao, chen zhuo ying fu, tao guang yang hui, you suo zuo wei*).

Drawing inspiration from PM Lee's call for "calm" and its similarities with Deng's *Tao Guang Yang Hui*, this article discusses the evolution of China's foreign policy since Deng Xiaoping, as well as the implications of this foreign policy transformation for Southeast Asia. Methodologically, this paper compares Deng Xiaoping's and Xi Jinping's foreign policy

[1] Pang Zhongying was a Visiting Senior Fellow at the ISEAS – Yusof Ishak Institute, Singapore. He is also a distinguished professor of International Relations at Ocean University of China in Qingdao. He would like to acknowledge the contributions of Lye Liang Fook (Coordinator and Senior Fellow of the Regional Strategic and Political Studies Programme at ISEAS) and Joel Chong (Research Associate with the Regional Strategic and Political Studies Programme at ISEAS) for their valuable input.

[2] Rei Kurohi, "Wuhan Virus: PM Lee Hsien Loong Calls for Calm, Urges Public Not to Spread Rumours", *Straits Times*, 28 January 2020, https://www.straitstimes.com/singapore/wuhan-virus-pm-lee-calls-for-calm-urges-public-not-to-spread-rumours

1

doctrines through an analysis of state narratives—namely the evolution from Deng's *Tao Guang Yang Hui* to Xi's *Xin Xing* (新型). This shift has largely been interpreted as the most important shift in China's foreign policy.

This paper will address three questions: Was Deng's *Tao Guang Yang Hui*, characterized by the "No's" (不: *bu*), really replaced? What is new about Xi's *Xin Xing*? And whither China's foreign policy?

UNPACKING *TAO GUANG YANG HUI*

Tao Guang Yang Hui, coined and formulated by Deng between 1989 and 1991, functioned as the core doctrine of China's foreign policy against the backdrop of the Tiananmen incident, the collapse of the Soviet Union, and the end of the Cold War. With *Tao Guang Yang Hui*, Deng relaunched China's "reform and opening up" with his well-known Southern Tour of 1992, and successfully froze China's internal debate on the "-isms"—i.e., socialism or capitalism—and re-embraced US-led globalization.

Today, "Deng Xiaoping Theory", which encompasses elements of *Tao Guang Yang Hui*, is enshrined in the People's Republic of China's Constitution, and accorded the same ideological standing as "Mao Zedong Thought" and "Xi Jinping Thought on Socialism with Chinese Characteristics for a New Era" as China's "guiding principles".

Tao Guang Yang Hui has been subject to a litany of differing interpretations from both inside and outside China. Ezra F. Vogel, the author of *Deng Xiaoping and the Transformation of China*, for instance writes: "Deng added an injunction to his successors about how to respond to continued Western sanctions and possible attacks: 'First,' he said, 'we should observe the situation coolly. Second, we should hold our ground. Third, we should act calmly. Don't be impatient. It is no good to be impatient. We should be calm, calm, and again calm, and quietly immerse ourselves in practical work to accomplish something— something for China.'"[3]

---

[3] Ezra F. Vogel, *Deng Xiaoping and the Transformation of China* (Cambridge, MA and London: Belknap of Harvard University Press, 2011), p. 646.

International interpretations of *Tao Guang Yang Hui*, including Vogel's, however, have been met with some resistance in China, highlighting the difference between international and domestic interpretations of the doctrine. The term has been officially translated in China as "keeping a low profile".[4] Some Chinese foreign policy figures such as General Xiong Guangkai (熊光楷), previously in charge of China's military diplomacy, have argued that the phrase's literal meaning is "to hide one's light and nourish oneself out of sight", with no element of "biding one's time". Xiong thus advocated that "hiding one's light" should be taken as *Tao Guang Yang Hui*'s most accurate translation.[5] Chinese interpretations such as Xiong's, however, have not been readily adopted by international scholars, with the mainstream international interpretation of *Tao Guang Yang Hui* remaining "hiding one's capabilities and biding one's time", or non-assertiveness.

However, in order to steer clear of this debate and obtain a better understanding of China's foreign policy doctrines, this paper examines official state discourses and narratives rather than international interpretations.

TAO GUANG YANG HUI AND THE NO's

The use of No's and Not's, or *bu*'s (不), occur frequently in narratives of China's foreign policy, and the doctrine of *Tao Guang Yang Hui* has likewise been articulated in this manner. Some important examples include:

- Will not challenge (不挑战: *bu tiao zhan*): In 1989, China reassured the United States, then the sole superpower, that it had no intention of challenging America's primacy in the world.

---

[4] Xuetong Yan, "From Keeping a Low Profile to Striving for Achievement", *Chinese Journal of International Politics* 7, issue 2 (Summer 2014): 153–84.

[5] 熊光楷, "'韬光养晦' 的中西误读", *FT* 中文网, 13 June 2010, http://www.ftchinese.com/story/001033110?archive

- Will not take the lead (不带头: *bu dai tou*): A principle of China's foreign policy since 1979, especially from 1989 to 2012.
- No export (不输出: *bu shu chu*): During the Deng years (1978–97) and thereafter till 2012, China became the largest trading nation in the global economy. Exporting mainly commodities, China stated that it would not export its political ideologies, including its "development model", as it "respects differences" with others.
- No hegemony (不称霸: *bu cheng ba*): China has repeatedly stated that it does not seek to be a global hegemon.
- China attaches "no political strings" (不附加条件: *bu fu jia tiao jian*) in its "development cooperation" with developing countries. The China International Development Cooperation Agency (CIDCA), established in 2018 as an integrated department to coordinate China's aid, often repeats this stance.[6]
- "No first use of nuclear weapons" (不首先使用: *bu shou xian shi yong*) is also one of China's international security principles.

It is worth noting that not every Chinese foreign policy principle is a No—some do not directly involve a No, but carry the essence of it. An example includes Deng's oft-cited "it doesn't matter if a cat is black or white, so long as it catches mice" (黑貓白貓能捉老鼠都是好貓). Deng's innovative "One Country, Two Systems" (一国两制*), with regard t*o Hong Kong, can also be treated as a unique No which excludes

---

[6] "No political strings attached" was first articulated by Zhou Enlai during his historic visit to Africa from 13 December 1963 to 5 February 1964. China continues to uphold this principle in its relations with "developing countries", particularly, with Asian and African nations. CIDCA was established in 2018 to integrate departments which were in the National Commission of Reform and Development, Commerce, MFA and others. It is now an independent agency, on par with "other ministries" or "other agencies". During the BRI summits in 2017 and 2019, the "no political strings attached" principle was restated by Xi and other leaders. However, it has also been criticized given that China has also asked others who received Chinese aid to acknowledge or recognize its "One China" principle.

any possibility of a change in Hong Kong's status for fifty years, after 1997.[7]

China's principle of "non-interference" has its roots in the Bandung Declaration, of which China is a signatory. China re-embraced the principle at the end of the Cultural Revolution, with Deng personally assuring Singapore's then Prime Minister Lee Kuan Yew of China's commitment to the principles of non-interference and non-intervention, during Deng's historic visit to Singapore in 1978. China thus committed itself to the pursuit of an "independent foreign policy of/for peace", from the late 1970s until the early 1980s, before the formulation of *Tao Guang Yang Hui*.

While the relevance of *Tao Guang Yang Hui* to Chinese foreign policy has waned since 2013, China has not completely abandoned its No's—some elements of *Tao Guang Yang Hui* has seemingly been kept.

The principle of "non-interference" continues to serve as an indispensable pillar of China-Southeast Asia relations. During his state visit to Myanmar on 17–18 January 2020, President Xi Jinping repeated "the five principles of mutual respect for sovereignty and territorial integrity, mutual non-aggression, non-interference in each other's internal affairs, equality and mutual benefit, and peaceful coexistence".[8]

In 2019, when the US Congress passed its Hong Kong Human Rights and Democracy Act,[9] China predictably invoked this principle of non-interference in protest—China's Foreign Affairs spokesperson Geng

---

[7] Article 5 of the People's Republic of China of The Basic Law of the Hong Kong Special Administrative Region: "The socialist system and policies shall not be practised in the Hong Kong Special Administrative Region, and the previous capitalist system and way of life shall remain unchanged for 50 years." See https://www.basiclaw.gov.hk/pda/en/basiclawtext/chapter_1.html

[8] Joint China-Myanmar Statement 中华人民共和国和缅甸联邦共和国, Ministry of Foreign Affairs of the People's Republic of China, 18 January 2020, https://www.fmprc.gov.cn/web/zyxw/t1733683.shtml

[9] https://www.congress.gov/bill/116th-congress/house-bill/3289

Shuang argued that the Act 'interfered' in China's domestic affairs, and that "Hong Kong affairs are purely China's internal affairs".[10]

These attempts at garnering international support for its position over issues like Hong Kong are needed to reaffirm China's national sovereignty and appease its domestic base. This is an emerging aspect of China's "non-interference" diplomacy. For example, China's foreign ministry stated, after South Korea President Moon Jae-in's visit to Beijing in December 2019, that the Republic of Korea recognizes Hong Kong as China's internal affairs. However, Seoul immediately corrected "China's version of President Moon's Hong Kong remarks", pointing out that Moon merely "noted" Xi's insistence that Hong Kong and Xinjiang were "internal affairs".[11]

Interestingly, as China shares this "non-interference" principle with several states in Asia, it has attempted to extend this principle to a regional level and to introduce "a Chinese version of an Asian regional security concept",[12] or "preventing external interference" (域外干涉: *yu wai gan she*) in the South China Sea.[13]

---

[10] "China Urges U.S. to Stop Meddling in Hong Kong Affairs", *Xinhua News Agency*, 19 September 2019, http://www.xinhuanet.com/english/2019-11/19/c_138567346.htm

[11] While it has been reported that South Korea "rejects" China's version of its President's remarks, "corrected" would be a more accurate descriptor. It is clear that South Korea does not want to be misinterpreted as supporting China's stance on Hong Kong, nor does it want to choose sides. Thus, Seoul was only clarifying, rather than rejecting what was represented by Beijing. See Kinling Lo, "South Korea Rejects China's Version of President Moon's Hong Kong Remarks", *South China Morning Post*, 25 December 2019, https://www.scmp.com/news/china/diplomacy/article/3043476/south-korea-rejects-chinas-version-president-moons-hong-kong

[12] Xi Jinping, "New Asian Security Concept for New Progress in Security Cooperation", Keynote Speech at 4th Conference on Interaction and Confidence Building Measures in Asia (CICA) Summit, Shanghai, 21 May 2014.

[13] "南海有了'准则'(COC)框架，域外干涉可休矣", *Xinhua News Agency*, 7 August 2017, http://xinhuanet.com/2017-08/07/c_1121445704.htm

Some argue that China's "non-interference" in regions such as Africa is over.[14] But, while its presence in Africa has increased, China has also renewed its No stances to Africa. For instance, China stated at the Beijing Summit of the Forum on China-Africa Cooperation (FOCAC) in September 2018 that it will take a five No's approach in its relations with the continent: "no interference in the development paths of individual countries; no interference in their internal affairs; no imposition of China's will; no attachment of political strings regarding assistance; and no seeking of selfish political gains in investment and financing cooperation".[15] This is also indicative that China's principle of "no hegemony" (不称霸: *bu cheng ba*) has taken on a new narrative of *Guo Qiang Bu Ba* (国强不霸), i.e. "a strong nation is not necessarily a hegemonic power" (中国绝不走'国强必霸'的路子).[16]

However, some of China's No's have disappeared or are no longer mentioned, or have been replaced by what China has termed the "New" (新型: *Xin Xing*). "Will not take the lead" (不带头: *bu dai tou*), for instance, has disappeared and been replaced with "international leadership with Chinese characteristics" under the guiding principles of *Yin Dao* (引导, see below). "No export" (不输出: *bu shu chu*) has been replaced by "experience sharing or providing" (为其他发展中国家提供经验和借鉴),[17] a de facto exportation of the "China Model' (中国模式) or the "Governance of China" (治国理政), which is now the principal projection of China's soft power in the world (see below).

---

[14] Obert Hodzi, *The End of China's Non-Intervention Policy in Africa* (Palgrave Macmillan, 2019).

[15] "China's 'Five-No' Approach Demonstrates Real Friendship Toward Africa: Kenyan Analyst", *Xinhua News Agency*, 6 September 2019, http://www.xinhuanet.com/english/2018-09/06/c_137447556.htm

[16] "China and the World in the New Era", White Paper 《新时代的中国与世界》白皮书, The Central People's Government of the People's Republic of China, 27 September 2019, http://www.gov.cn/zhengce/2019-09/27/content_5433889.htm

[17] Ibid.

FROM *TAO GUANG YANG HUI* TO *XIN XING*

Before any discussion of China's current foreign policy, one has to consider its transition from *Tao Guang Yang Hui* to its current *Xin Xing*, the latter of which was implemented in 2013. This transition began in 2002/2003, at the start of the Hu Jintao era.

A key development in this process was the formulation of the "peaceful rise" narrative by Zheng Bijian, former vice president of the Communist Party of China's Central Party School.[18] While the discourse of China's "peaceful rise" has been studied extensively, few have noticed Zheng's reluctance to refer to China as a "power". China has also intentionally avoided the use of the term "power", favouring the term "major country" (大国: *da guo*, or 世界大国: *shi jie da guo*) over "major power". For example, China proposed that its state-to-state relationship with the United States be termed "major country relations" (大国关系: *da guo guan xi*) rather than "major power relations". The "peaceful rise" narrative thus represents an early attempt at transforming *Tao Guang Yang Hui* into the defining doctrine of Hu Jintao's foreign policy. Its original intention was not a departure from *Tao Guang Yang Hui*, but a revision of it to suit China's growing presence on the world stage.

This revised term contributed to the shift in China's foreign policy under Hu Jintao. However, its element of "rise" did not sit well with Hu, who favoured Deng's "will not challenge" (不挑战: *bu tiao zhan*) approach. "Will not challenge" was part of a larger Deng strategy that emphasized that "the megatrends of the world are peace and development", and that "China can seize the opportunity to concentrate on its economic development". Deng wanted no wars between the great powers, and instead focused on "economic development" rather than

---

[18] Zheng Bijian, "China's 'Peaceful Rise' to Great-Power Status", *Foreign Affairs* 84, no. 5 (September–October 2005): 22. The Brookings Institution published Zheng Bijian's collection titled *China's Peaceful Rise: Speeches 1997–2004*, https://www.brookings.edu/wp-content/uploads/2012/04/20050616bijianlunch.pdf

"rise".[19] Therefore, I regard the "peaceful rise" discourse as only a minor tentative paradigm change. The decade under Hu was thus largely a continuation of Deng's *Tao Guang Yang Hui*. Hu's leadership instead focused on showcasing China's "peaceful development path"—the only point of departure from Deng's "peace and development".[20]

In 2013, as the world debated the legacy of Hu Jintao's foreign policy, China's foreign policy transformation was only beginning to be discussed internationally. Related to this, I contributed the paper "Does China Need a New Foreign Policy?" to a SIPRI conference in Stockholm, Sweden entitled "The Hu Jintao Decade in China's Foreign and Security Policy". In the paper, I argued that China's current foreign policy would be maintained albeit with certain necessary changes, in response to international onlookers who argued that China was possibly embracing a new foreign policy.[21]

On the other hand, China's foreign policy transformation has been a hot topic of discussion within China's mainstream international/foreign policy studies community since 2008, the year when China organized the Beijing Olympics and joined the 1st G20 summit in Washington, DC. Discussion on the topic peaked, however, around 2014–15. A simple Google search demonstrates this:

- Yaqing Qin, "Continuity through Change: Background Knowledge and China's International Strategy", *Chinese Journal of International Politics* 7, issue 3 (Autumn 2014): 285–314.

---

[19] "Peace and Development Are the Two Outstanding Issues in the World Today", *Selected Works of Deng Xiaoping (1982–1992)*, vol. 3 (Beijing: Renmin Press, 2001), pp. 105, 127, 344, 383.

[20] "中国和平发展道路", Ministry of Foreign Affairs of the People's Republic of China, 24 August 2006, https://www.fmprc.gov.cn/web/ziliao_674904/tytj_674911/zcwj_674915/t24780.shtml, and "中国的和平发展", The Central People's Government of the People's Republic of China, 6 September 2011, http://www.gov.cn/zwgk/2011-09/06/content_1941258.htm

[21] The Hu Jintao Decade in China's Foreign and Security Policy (2002-2012): Assessments and Implications, Draft Agenda, http://nias.asia/sites/default/files/images/2013_sipri_conference_on_contemporary_china-2.pdf

- Sun Xuefeng, M. Taylor Fravel, and Liu Feng, "Understanding China's Foreign Policy Transformation: A *CJIP* Reader", *Chinese Journal of International Politics* 7 (2014).
- Daniel C. Lynch, *China's Futures: PRC Elites Debate Economics, Politics, and Foreign Policy* (Stanford: Stanford University Press, 2015).
- Shao Binhong, *China Under Xi Jinping: Its Economic Challenges and Foreign Policy Initiatives* (Brill, 2015).
- Zhu Feng and Lu Peng, "Be Strong and Be Good? Continuity and Change in China's International Strategy under Xi Jinping", *China Quarterly of International Strategic Studies* 1, no. 1 (2015).

Chinese scholars discussed the topic intensely. Indeed, the first seminar organized by the newly established "social" think-tank Intellisia Institution (海国图智研究院) in Shenzhen was on the "Transformation of China's Foreign Policy" (中国外交转型) from 19 to 20 December 2015. Several such seminars were also held in Beijing and Shanghai.

XIN XING CHARACTERISTICS IN THE "NEW ERA"

Like *Tao Guang Yang Hui* before it, *Xin Xing* (新型, or "new type/model") has come to gradually dominate the narrative of China's foreign policy; at the same time, the end of *Tao Guang Yang Hui* was never officially declared. Many *Xin Xing* for the "new era" (新时代: *xin shi dai*) were formulated under Xi Jinping:

- China described itself as a "new major country" (新型大国: *xin xing da guo*).[22]

---

[22] As pointed out in this piece, China's official translation (by its Ministry of Foreign Affairs) is "major country" rather than "great power".

- China practised "new international relations" (新型国际关系: *xin xing guo ji guan xi*), particularly, "new major country relations" (新型大国关系: *xin xing da guo guan xi*).
- China formulated a "new neighbourhood policy" for a "new regional order" in Asia. China's "neighbourhood foreign policy work conference" produced the new concepts of "amity, sincerity, mutual benefit, and inclusiveness" (亲、诚、惠、容: *qin, cheng, hui, rong*).[23] In 2013, two unprecedented projects were sponsored by China: the unilateral One Belt One Road (OBOR) (一带一路) project[24] and the multilateral Asian Infrastructure Investment Bank (AIIB) project. Zhang Yunling argued that "China's regional conception based on its surrounding areas has made a comeback and China has made great efforts to rebuild the relations and order with new thinking and new approaches" (中国的周边区域观回归与新秩序构建).[25]
- In 2017, during the 19th CPC Congress, China formally proposed a "new outlook of global governance" (新型全球治理观: *xin xing quan qiu zhi li guan*) for the first time, declaring that China provides "new public goods" (新型公共产品: *xin xing gong gong chan pin*) regionally and globally.

Most of China's new narratives of foreign policy is prefixed with "new", although the most important of its new foreign policy principles, "a community with a shared future for mankind" (人类命运共同体: *ren lei ming yun gong tong ti*, RLMYGTT) is not. Essentially, this principle argues that it is in the interest of countries in the world to come together

---

[23] "习近平在周边外交工作座谈会上发表重要讲话", *Xinhua News Agency*, 25 October 2013, http://www.xinhuanet.com/politics/2013-10/25/c_117878897. htm

[24] This was initially officially translated from Chinese to English as "One Belt and One Road" (OBOR), a term adopted by international stakeholders.

[25] 张蕴岭, "中国的周边区域观回归与新秩序构建", 世界经济与政治, 2015年第1期.

to work on initiatives that will bring about mutual benefits, given the interdependence and interconnectedness of the world. The oft-cited example is the Belt and Road Initiative (BRI), which although unilaterally initiated by China, would require the participation and ownership of other countries in order for mutual benefits to be reaped. This need for cooperation is in line with what China regards as the current broad trends of peace, development, and cooperation. In particular, China has called on countries and organizations to band together to fight COVID-19, which is continuing its scourge around the world. In early February 2020, at the height of the coronavirus outbreak in China, its ambassador to the United States Cui Tiankai reiterated that RLMYGTT was at "the core of China's foreign policy".[26] He further said that the "fight against the coronavirus outbreak shows again that we live in a shared community where all of us are interlinked and interdependent. Countries must join hands to cope with the difficulties and challenges they face. Actually, the world has seen similar situations, such as the H1N1 virus, Ebola and many other health challenges. Facts prove that no matter how difficult the case may be, as long as we all work together as members of the international community and in the spirit of solidarity, we will succeed in curbing the disease and saving lives".[27] Ambassador Cui also underscored the importance for the United States and China to work together not only in fighting COVID-19 but also in many other areas of common interest.

CHINA AND SOUTHEAST ASIA

Southeast Asia was the first region in which China sought to implement RLMYGTT. As opposed to the Deng Xiaoping, Jiang Zemin, and Hu Jintao years, the United States is no longer regarded to be among the "priority of priorities" (重中之重: *zhong zhong zhi zhong*) in China's

---

[26] "Remarks by Ambassador Cui Tiankai At the Forum on US-China Relations", Embassy of the People's Republic of China in the United States of America, 2 February 2020, http://www.china-embassy.org/eng/zmgxss/t1738974.htm

[27] Ibid.

foreign policy. China's "surrounding areas" (周边: *zhou bian*), or neighbourhood diplomacy, have instead become a major priority.

In January 2020, during President Xi Jinping's visit to Myanmar, both countries agreed to "jointly build [a] community with [a] shared future".[28] Before this trip, China had already signed two RLMYGTT agreements in Southeast Asia:

- "China-Laos relations as a model of RLMYGTT" (中老作为"示范": *zhong lao zuo wei "shi fan"*): On 30 April 2019, during the second Belt and Road Forum in Beijing, Xi Jinping and Bounnhang Vorachith signed an RLMYGTT agreement between the Chinese Communist Party and the Lao People's Revolutionary Party (关于构建中老命运共同体行动计划).[29] Song Yinhui indicated then that more of such bilateral agreements would follow.[30]

- On 28 April 2019, China and Cambodia signed an "Action Plan 2019–2023 on Building China-Cambodia Community of Shared Future" (构建中柬命运共同体行动计划) in Beijing during Cambodian Prime Minister Hun Sen's attendance at the second Belt and Road Forum.[31] PM Hun Sen further visited Beijing in February 2020, amid the worsening coronavirus crisis in Wuhan. The visit was praised as the Cambodian leader practising RLMYGTT: "The visit has shown

---

[28] Poppy McPherson, Ruma Paul, and Shoonhina Struggles in New Diplomatic Role, Trying to Return Rohingya to Myanmar", *Reuters*, 20 January 2020, https://www.reuters.com/article/us-myanmar-rohingya-china-insight/china-struggles-in-new-diplomatic-role-trying-to-return-rohingya-to-myanmar-idUSKBN1ZJ0SY

[29] "规划两国长远发展时间表路线图中国老挝签命运共同体计划", *Lianhe Zaobao*, 2 May 2019, https://www.zaobao.com.sg/news/china/story20190502-953137

[30] "中国老挝签署命运共同体行动计划开启双边关系新时代", *Xinhua News Agency*, 1 May 2019, http://www.xinhuanet.com/world/2019-05/01/c_1124440741.htm

[31] "China-Cambodia Community of Shared Future Features Four Special Points: Chinese Ambassador to Cambodia", *Fresh News*, 28 April 2020, http://en.freshnewsasia.com/index.php/en/localnews/13941-2019-05-08-08-06-23.html

the core meaning of a community with a shared future for China and Cambodia."[32]

Furthermore, on the 70th anniversary of the People's Liberation Army Navy (PLAN) on 23 April 2019 in Qingdao, Xi Jinping called for the maritime dimension of the RLMYGTT (海洋命运共同体: *hai yang ming yun gong tong ti*). At this event, Xi appeared to send a timely message of peace to not only Southeast Asia, but also other players such as Japan and South Korea, whose naval representatives were present. China was keen to collaborate with other countries to combat non-traditional security threats such as piracy—the Chinese navy, for instance, had been patrolling in the Gulf of Aden and in waters off the coast of Somalia in the western Indian Ocean region, since late 2008. However, the maritime dimension of the RLMYGTT has been ignored regionally and globally. After Xi's speech, China organized numerous discussions to create a roadmap of the concept.

While it is unclear whether China applies both RLMYGTT, the professed "core of China's foreign policy", and its maritime variant to issues such as the South China Sea and ongoing COC negotiations with ASEAN, scholars such as Peking University international relations professor Zhai Kun have argued that it is important for China to practise what it preaches.[33]

In addition to RLMYGTT, the following are new discourses which are without the *Xin Xing* prefix.

Firstly, while China has continued to invoke "non-interference" under *Xin Xing*, it has also begun to explore international intervention "with Chinese characteristics". After the 19th CCP Congress in October

---

[32] Baijie An, "Xi: Nation Can Win Battle Against Virus", *China Daily*, 6 February 2020, https://www.chinadaily.com.cn/a/202002/06/WS5e3b10b5a3101282172753da.html

[33] Zhai Kun argues that China's actions have to mirror its stated principles (知行合一: *zhi xing he yi*). See "翟崑：海洋命运共同体构建需知行合一", Academy of Ocean of China, 18 March 2020, https://aoc.ouc.edu.cn/_t719/2020/0318/c9821a282413/page.htm

2017, in discussing China's "new major country" diplomacy, the term "constructive intervention" (建设性介入: *jian she xing jie ru*) was mentioned and stressed by Wang Yi, the current State Councillor and Foreign Minister.[34] Some Chinese scholars, including this author, have argued that China needs to address its "non-intervention question" in order to adopt a "strictly conditional interventionist" policy.[35] Wang Yizhou, for instance, argued that China should conduct "creative involvement diplomacy".[36] However, "constructive intervention" or "creative involvement" has now seemingly been replaced by the more moderate narrative of "constructive role", as evidenced by China's role in Myanmar's peace process. In particular, China has appointed a special envoy to focus on Myanmar affairs since 2013 and has tried to broker peace among the various armed ethnic minority groups in Myanmar via the Panglong Peace Conference.[37]

Secondly, under *Xin Xing*, China has also sought an international leading role (引导: *yin dao*). The term *Yin Dao* has drawn differing interpretations—some have argued that China seeks leadership on the global stage, while others have pointed out that the concept should not be viewed so ambitiously as China is only seeking to increase its role in

---

[34] "在2017年国际形势与中国外交研讨会开幕式上的演讲", Ministry of Foreign Affairs of the People's Republic of China, 9 December 2017, https://www.fmprc.gov.cn/web/wjbzhd/t1518042.shtml

[35] Pang Zhongying, "The Non-interference Dilemma: Adapting China's Approach to the New Context of African and International Realities", in *China-Africa Relations: Governance, Peace and Security*, edited by Mulugeta Gebrehiwot Berhe (Institute for Peace and Security Studies, Addis Ababa University, 2013).

[36] 王逸舟: 《创造性介入: 中国外交新取向》, 北京大学出版社, 2011年 and its English edition: Wang Yizhou, *Creative Involvement: A New Direction of China's Diplomacy* (Taylor & Francis, 2017).

[37] Teddy Ng and Minnie Chan, "Beijing's First Special Envoy for Asia to Focus on Myanmar", *South China Morning Post*, 12 March 2013, https://www.scmp.com/news/china/article/1188814/beijings-first-special-envoy-asia-focus-myanmar, and "2nd Round of Myanmar Peace Talks Begins as China Brings 'Soft Power' to Process", *Mizzima*, 25 May 2017, http://www.mizzima.com/news-domestic/2nd-round-myanmar-peace-talks-begins-china-brings-%25E2%2580%2598soft-power%25E2%2580%2599-process

major international processes or crisis management.[38] Officially, *Yin Dao* refers to not only a general leadership in the inter-state system, but also what President Xi Jinping has mentioned "for the very first time"[39] as China's "two leading roles (两个引导) policy", with the "two" referring to China playing a leading role in shaping the new world order and international security."[40]

Thirdly, China frequently talks about "international public goods" (国际公共产品: *guo ji gong gong chan pin*). The concept of "international public goods" was initially confined to scholarly debates in China, but later became the principal instrument through which China sought to implement RLMYGTT. A constant official refrain is that China has offered "facilities available to all nations and peoples in the South China Sea" (such as lighthouses, maritime observation, meteorological forecasting, environmental monitoring, and disaster prevention and reduction facilities) although China has also faced criticism over its provision of such "public goods".[41]

---

[38] From an "experimental leader" (one that is testing the waters) to one where China seeks to play a leading role. The term "experimental leader" was coined by Prof Jia Qingguo in "The Shanghai Cooperation Organization: China's Experiment in Multilateral Leadership", *Japan SRC Hokudai* 16 (2015), http://src-h.slav.hokudai.ac.jp/coe21/publish/no16_2_ses/05_jia.pdf.

[39] Matteo Dian, Silvia Menegazzi, *New Regional Initiatives in China's Foreign Policy: The Incoming Pluralism of Global Governance* (Palgrave Macmillan, 2018), p. 26.

[40] For an authoritative Chinese source of the "Two Guides (两个引导)", see "习近平首提'两个引导'有深意", *Sohu*, 20 February 2020, http://news.sohu.com/20170220/n481236636.shtml?qq-pf-to=pcqq.group. See also Zheping Huang, "Chinese President Xi Jinping Has Vowed to Lead the 'New World Order'", *Quartz*, 22 February 2017, https://qz.com/916382/chinese-president-xi-jinping-has-vowed-to-lead-the-new-world-order/

[41] Zhang Mingliang, "China's Development of Public Goods in the South China Sea Islands", in *China's Globalization and the Belt and Road Initiative*, edited by J. Berlie (Palgrave Macmillan, 2020), pp. 101–22. See also "Full text of Chinese Premier Li Keqiang's Speech at China-ASEAN Summit", *Xinhua News Agency*, 15 November 2018, http://www.xinhuanet.com/english/2018-11/15/c_137607654.htm

Joseph Nye noted that "Charles Kindleberger, one of the intellectual architects of the Marshall Plan, argued that the disastrous decade of the 1930s was a result of the United States' failure to provide global public goods after it had replaced Britain as the leading power. Today, as China's power grows, will it make the same mistake?"[42] It may be the case that China is trying to address its differences/disputes with neighbouring nations by providing more public goods. In addition to the above-mentioned provision of public goods related to the South China Sea, China has also been regarding the Belt and Road Initiative (BRI) as a public good since its inception.[43] China has further proposed the concept of "bandwagoning" (搭车: *da che*), that calls on countries in the world to join China's Belt and Road "bandwagon" so that they can together benefit from being part of this initiative. For instance, on 22 August 2014, Xi Jinping said in Ulaanbaatar: "You can take a ride on our express train," for China-Mongolia "joint development".[44] On 7 November 2015, at the 36th Singapore Lecture, Xi further elaborated on his "China ride" theory: "China welcomes its neighbours to board the fast train of China's development."[45] However, China seems to have overlooked the contradiction of such bandwagoning with its adherence to the "non-alliance" principle or the principle of not forming a formal alliance relationship with other countries. A potential solution is China's "partnership theory", which advocates forming partnerships for mutual benefits, as distinct from an alliance relationship (结伴而不结盟).

---

[42] Joseph Nye, "The Kindleberger Trap", Belfer Center for Science and International Affairs, 9 January 2017, https://www.belfercenter.org/publication/kindleberger-trap

[43] "The BRI Is a Global Public Goods", China Center for International Economic Exchanges, 15 June 2017, http://www.cciee.org.cn/Detail.aspx?newsId=13859&TId=231

[44] Teddy Ng, "Xi Says China Respects Mongolia's Independence, but Stresses Joint Development", *South China Morning Post*, 23 August 2014, https://www.scmp.com/news/china/article/1579609/take-ride-our-express-train-xi-jinping-tells-mongolia

[45] Jinping Xi, *The 36th Singapore Lecture: Forging A Strong Partnership To Enhance Prosperity of Asia* (Singapore: ISEAS – Yusof Ishak Institute, 2015).

Fourthly, under *Xin Xing*, "no export" has been replaced by the export of the "China model" of development and governance to the world, especially the developing world. The predecessor of the "China model" is the "Beijing Consensus", a term coined not by China's ruling party or its public policy institutions but by US journalist Joshua Cooper Ramo. Ramo, vice-chairman and co-chief executive of Kissinger Associates, coined the concept in a report by the Foreign Policy Centre: "China has discovered its own economic consensus".[46] Some international scholars who have worked and lived in China have also contributed to the emergence of this "China model". Daniel A. Bell, the author of *The China Model: Political Meritocracy and the Limits of Democracy*, is an example.[47] The 18th and 19th CPC Congresses in 2012 and 2017 reaffirmed this as "the Governance of China" (中国之治: *zhong guo zhi zhi*). China has been actively exporting its development and governance model since this official endorsement.[48]

I argue that *Xin Xing* narratives, especially RLMYGTT, have defined the nature of the export of the "China model". Materially, BRI investments from China contain the fundamental "China model" in economics; ideationally, as RLMYGTT is defined by a "shared future", the sharedness implies the exportation of the "China model". Therefore, the exportation of the "China model" is an indispensable element of RLMYGTT. Although China has reassured Africa and the rest of Asia that it respects their "choice of development path", China has continued to share its development experience and approaches with countries in both continents. In particular, Xi's book, *The Governance of China*, a

---

[46] Joshua Cooper Ramo, "China Has Discovered Its Own Economic Consensus", The Foreign Policy Centre, 8 May 2004, https://fpc.org.uk/wp-content/uploads/2006/09/240-1.pdf

[47] Bell has been the dean of the School of Politics and Public Administration at Shandong University in Qingdao since 2017.

[48] Elizabeth Economy, "Yes, Virginia, China Is Exporting Its Model", Council on Foreign Relations, 11 December 2019, https://www.cfr.org/blog/yes-virginia-china-exporting-its-model

collection of Xi's speeches that underline Xi's political philosophy and strategic guidelines for the conduct of China's domestic development and foreign policy, which has been published in two volumes and subsequently translated into various languages for circulation, is a typical example of China sharing its development model with other countries. It, in some sense, can be regarded as a projection of China's soft power.

If we examine China's projection of soft power under the *Xin Xing* framework together with its export of the "China model", it is obvious that China is no longer satisfied with just "cultural soft power" (中国文化软实力), a phrase which was commonly used under President Hu Jintao.[49] Under Xi, China is no longer satisfied with the pursuit of soft power that is merely confined to the cultural realm, but wants to expand it further to include a political dimension, namely the projection of its development (发展经验) and governance (治国理政) models.[50] This is a fundamental shift.

A 3As FRAMEWORK?

China's foreign policy transformation is driven by three forces, in what this paper calls the 3As framework. The first A is Ambition. Since 2013, under Xi's "China Dream" (中国梦), China has been striving to correct what I call the "imperfectness" of *Tao Guang Yang Hui*, and to ambitiously formulate a *Xin Xing*/new foreign policy to fit its self-declared "great country" status (大国地位: *da guo di wei*). *Tao Guang*

---

[49] In the early 2000s, China discovered the importance of soft power and decided to not only learn the concept of "soft power" from the United States but also address this issue at the 16th CCP Party Congress in 2002. A key manifestation of China's cultural soft power projection then was the establishment of Confucius Institutes around the world.

[50] I delivered a keynote lecture on China's cultural diplomacy in Africa at Germany's Frankfurt University in 2013, which hosts a Confucius Institute co-run by the Fudan University in Shanghai and the Goethe University in Frankfurt. See http://www.afraso.org/en/content/confucius-institute-afraso-lecture-opening-china%E2%80%99s-cultural-diplomacy-africa-%E2%80%93-recent

Yang Hui and its series of No's during the 1990s and 2000s was seen as a foreign policy that was self-constrained or imperfect, and Xi's "great country" foreign policy attempts to correct this. If the stage guided by *Tao Guang Yang Hui* was China's "have-not" foreign policy, then *Xin Xing* can be seen as China's "have" foreign policy.[51]

The second A is Alternatives. China's ambitiousness was pursued via a number of unprecedented big "alternatives", ranging from the unilateral BRI to its multilateral AIIB-like sponsorship. The AIIB was not designed to replace but to complement existing international development financing institutions such as the World Bank and Asian Development Bank, although it has strong potential to be an "alternative". Originally, the Shanghai-based New Development Bank or BRICS Bank was formed as a "mini" alternative to the US-dominated World Bank.[52]

China's foreign policy ambitions and its proposed alternatives has led to international concern over "China's challenge", "China's assertiveness", "China as a revisionist power" as well as concerns about a "Chinese world order". However, these concerns do not take into account China's demonstrated willingness to adapt and adjust the manner and tone of its international engagement. Such concerns thus exaggerate China's ambitions on the global stage.

The third A is Adaptation. On the foreign policy front, some Chinese diplomats have seemingly taken on an increasingly strident and aggressive "Wolf Warrior" approach in defending China's interests.[53]

---

[51] "庞中英:中国外交的'不'与'有'", *Aisixiang*, 9 July 2015, http://www.aisixiang.com/data/90304.html

[52] Yu Shujun, "An Alternative Model of Development Finance", *Beijing Review*, No. 39, 29 September 2016.

[53] For an analysis of this "Wolf Warrior" approach, see Sarah Zhang, "China's Wolf Warrior Diplomats Battle on Twitter for Control of Coronavirus Narrative", *South China Morning Post*, 23 March 2020, https://www.scmp.com/news/china/diplomacy/article/3076384/chinas-wolf-warriors-battle-twitter-control-coronavirus

Recent examples of this approach include remarks made by China spokesperson Zhao Lijian and its ambassador to France Lu Shaye, both of whom have taken a combative stance when questioned about the source of the coronavirus. This more combative approach can be regarded as China adapting and responding to what it perceives as other countries' unfair criticism of China, and China's desire to be accorded respect commensurate with its current global status.[54]

The above examples show that China is constantly monitoring and adapting to a rapidly changing and unpredictable world. A mantra of China's ruling party is to "monitor the situation, anticipate changes" (审时度势: *shen shi du shi*). This adaptability is typified by Xi's *Da Bian Ju* narrative, i.e., "the world today is going through changes of a kind unseen in a century" (当今世界正经历百年未有之大变局).[55] Since 2017, the *Da Bian Ju* narrative has guided China's "new adaptation" to its changing external environment. That is why *Xin Xing* has to coexist with the No's—in fact, Deng's *Tao Guang Yang Hui* has survived in different ways and forms. In the *Xin Xing* era, China's foreign policy does not lack the flexibility needed to adapt to a complex world, characterised by *Da Bian Ju*.

I argue that China, as a state actor, is one that is still learning to navigate the international system. The OBOR's reformulation as the BRI is a meaningful example. It is no longer rhetorically a "strategy" ("strategy" signifying "ambition" and "hidden intentions") but just an "initiative", demonstrating a high degree of pragmatism. As Lee Jones and Jinghan Zeng note, the BRI is not China's grand strategy but "an extremely loose, indeterminate scheme, driven primarily by competing domestic

---

[54] There are others such as China's ambassador to the United States Cui Tiankai, who comes across as being more rational and level-headed.

[55] Yang Jiechi (杨洁篪), "Working Together to Meet Our Shared Responsibility and Build a Community with a Shared Future for Mankind" (携手同心，共担责任，努力推动构建人类命运共同体), a keynote speech at the 18th Beijing Forum, 1 November 2019, http://www.uscnpm.com/model_item.html?action=view&table=article&id=19946

interests, particularly state capitalist interests, whose struggle for power and resources are already shaping BRI's design and implementation".[56]

Other examples of China's adaption in its ideological narratives include China's "constructive intervention/involvement", outlined in the political report of the 18th CPC Congress in 2012, which was revised to a "constructive role" after the 19th CPC Congress in 2017. Most importantly, the official translation of RLMYGTT was changed from "community of common destiny" (first termed as such in 2012 and again in 2017) to "community with a shared future" on 1 December 2018,[57] when Xi spoke at the CPC in Dialogue with World Political Parties High-Level Meeting.[58] This change from "common destiny" to "shared future" demonstrates how it is possible for China to adapt and adjust its ideological narratives for its external audience.[59] However, in Zhang Fa's view, although the word "future" is a much better formulation than the word "destiny", both do not adequately reflect the original meaning of the Chinese words Ming Yun (命运).[60]

---

[56] L. Jone and J. Zeng, "Understanding China's 'Belt and Road Initiative': Beyond 'Grand Strategy' to a State Transformation Analysis", 2018, https://www.tandfonline.com/doi/abs/10.1080/01436597.2018.1559046

[57] "Xi Jinping's Keynote Speech at the CPC in Dialogue With World Political Parties High-Level Meeting", *China Insight*, 1 December 2017, http://www.bjreview.com/CHINA_INSIGHT/Special_Edition/201802/t20180212_800117836.html

[58] "Community of Common Destiny" was already in use by the international community before the translation was revised. For example, in a 2018 discussion on "China's proposal for an ASEAN-China community of common destiny", Hoang Thi Ha used the term's abbreviation "CCD". See Hoang Thi Ha, "Understanding China's Proposal for an ASEAN-China Community of Common Destiny and ASEAN's Ambivalent Response", *Contemporary Southeast Asia* 41, no. 2 (August 2019).

[59] This translational change illustrates how China has realized that it is difficult to forge a "common destiny" with others, and instead now chooses to address the "future". However, as argued by Professor Zhang Fa (张法), "future" loses the originality of "命运共同体", highlighting the contradictions and dilemmas that come with conceptualizing and implementing this *Xin Xing* foreign policy.

[60] 張法, "命 運觀的中、西、印比較——從 '人類命運共同體' 英譯難點談起", 《南國學術》 (Nan Guo Xue Shu), 澳門大學 (University of Macau), no. 5, 2019, p. 266.

WHITHER CHINA'S COMPLEX FOREIGN POLICY?

Nonetheless, Chinese grand strategist and historian Shi Yinhong (时殷弘) argues that "China [has begun] to come up with a grand strategy in its foreign relations". He regards the BRI as encompassing a "strategic economy" (战略经济: *zhan lue jing ji*) element as well as other "strategies", such as the "strategic military" (战略军事: *zhan lue jun shi*) element.[61] He additionally argued in 2016 that China could risk facing a "strategic overreach" (中国"战略透支"风险日增).[62] China clearly ignored warnings of this risk and continued to expand its physical and strategic presence in the past several years since the formal launch of the BRI in 2013.

It will be hard for China's existing "governance system and governance capacity" to support and sustain this overreach. The communique of the 19th CPC Central Committee's 4th plenary session on 31 October 2019 stated the need "to advance the modernization of China's system and capacity for governance".[63] Of course, this new "modernization" is absolutely not about "political modernization" or "political reform", but the "modernization" of China's governance system and capabilities. CPC leadership has even acknowledged that the outbreak of COVID-19 is a "big test" (大考: *da kao*) for China's "governance system and governance capacity". [64]

---

[61] Shi Yinhong, (时殷弘), "China's complicated foreign policy", ECFR, 31 March 2015, http://www.ecfr.eu/article/commentary_chinas_complicated_foreign_policy311562

[62] 蔡永伟, "时殷弘教授: 中国'战略透支'风险日增", *Lianhe Zaobao*, 21 September 2016, https://www.zaobao.com.sg/znews/greater-china/story20160921-668655

[63] "19th CPC Central Committee concludes fourth plenary session, releases communique", *Xinhua News Agency*, 31 October 2019, http://www.xinhuanet.com/english/2019-10/31/c_138518832.htm

[64] "Xi chairs leadership meeting on epidemic control" *Xinhua News Agency*, 3 February 2020, http://www.xinhuanet.com/english/2020-02/03/c_138753250.htm

In the fight against COVID-19, especially in its initial stages, China's overcentralized political system was seen as being slow to respond to the outbreak in Wuhan. The pandemic has also provoked a strong backlash from some countries, who have pointed to China as the source of the coronavirus and also criticized its initial handling of the outbreak. In view of these negative international reactions and the seeming limitations of an overcentralized political system, some Chinese observers are of the view that China will not be able to continue with the wholesale implementation of its *Xin Xing* foreign policy. They believe that China's foreign policy is likely to see some adjustments in the post-COVID period.

In particular, a seasoned political observer at a Chinese think-tank opined that it is time for China to strategically, or at least tactically, take a lower profile on the world stage and re-embrace elements of *Tao Guang Yang Hui*.[65] There could be some validity to such a view. Firstly, China will need to pay more attention domestically to restart or rebuild the momentum of economic growth battered by COVID-19, that has resulted in enterprise bankruptcies and closures, rising unemployment, and the relocation or further diversification of production networks. Secondly, trade, which has been the foundation of China's economic growth, has been severely hit by the deterioration in US-China relations, and the benefits of BRI has so far been unable to make up for the importance of the American market to China. The blame game between the world's two major powers has continued, and this does not bode well for their future relationship. This will also have implications for other countries. Thirdly, China's relations with countries such as the EU, UK, and Australia are likely to become more difficult due primarily to their perception of how China had mishandled the COVID-19 outbreak in Wuhan. Fourthly, Asian and African countries, who are key participants in the BRI, are likely to request to rework or even delay their loan repayment arrangements vis-à-vis China. This will worsen China's international debt situation and further dampen prospects for its economy.

---

[65] The author's interview with a seasoned Chinese political watcher on 25 February 2020.

However, it appears that China is continuing with its current trajectory of strategic overreach, seemingly unstopped by the COVID-19 crisis. Xi, during his visit to Myanmar on 17 January 2020, vowed to accelerate the China-Myanmar Economic Corridor (CMEC), which is seen by both sides as a key project in their BRI collaboration.[66] Amid the public health crisis, Xi received two Asian leaders in Beijing to stress the continuation of the BRI and the "building of a community of shared future"—Cambodian PM Hun Sen visited Beijing on 4 February 2020 and Mongolian President Khaltmaa Battulga on 27 February 2020. On 20 February 2020, the 5th Lancang-Mekong Cooperation Foreign Ministers' Meeting was held in Vientiane, Laos. China seeks to connect the LMC with the "New International Land-Sea Trade Corridor" (国际陆海贸易新通道) to form the "Lancang-Mekong Cooperation Economic Development Belt", which has been touted as a combination of "One Belt" and "One Road".[67] However, the negative growth in China in first quarter 2020, the first time this has happened since its open door and reform policy in 1978, and which is due primarily to the coronavirus crisis, has made the future of the BRI uncertain.[68]

China has refused to see the containment of the coronavirus as a failure in governance, but as a success. It has declared that it had

---

[66] Wang Yi, "On Xi Jinping's Visit to Myanmar", Ministry of Foreign Affairs of the People's Republic of China, 19 January 2020, https://www.fmprc.gov.cn/web/zyxw/t1733789.shtml, and Lye Liang Fook, "China's Emphasis on Ties with Southeast Asia", *ISEAS Commentaries*, 2020/10, 22 January 2020, https://www.iseas.edu.sg/media/commentaries/chinas-emphasis-on-ties-with-southeast-asia-by-lye-liang-fook/

[67] The Joint Press Communiqué of the Fifth Mekong-Lancang Cooperation Foreign Ministers' Meeting, Ministry of Foreign Affairs of the People's Republic of China, 20 February 2020, http://www.fmcoprc.gov.hk/eng/Topics/gjfz/t1748085.htm

[68] China's economy shrank for the first time in more than forty years, in the first quarter of 2020. See Thomas Hale, Xinning Liu, and Yuan Yang "China's Economy Shrinks for First Time in Four Decades", *Financial Times*, 17 April 2020, https://www.ft.com/content/8f941520-67ad-471a-815a-d6ba649d22ed

successfully used its "institutional/system advantage" (举国体制: *ju guo ti zhi*), its centralized system led by the Chinese Communist Party, to overcome the pandemic at home. China has even provided extensive aid to other countries and continents to fight the pandemic. China sees itself as being in a position to provide a "China model" in containing the coronavirus,[69] and also further promotes the principle of RLMYGTT when it collaborates with others in fighting the virus.[70]

Whither China's *Xin Xing* foreign policy? There are two possibilities. First, China's *Xin Xing* foreign policy will continue as before, where China will run the risk of strategic overreach, more intense competition with the United States, and rising concerns from other countries over China's intentions. Second, it may be possible that China could either re-embrace a revised *Tao Guang Yang Hui* under *Xin Xing*, or it could make adjustments to its current *Xin Xing* foreign policy to bring it closer to a twenty-first century *Tao Guang Yang Hui*, to mitigate its rivalry with the United States and allay somewhat the concerns of other countries. It is not at all clear which alternative China will take at this juncture.

---

[69] "Xinhua Headlines: China's Anti-Virus Efforts Pilot Model in Building Community with Shared Future", *Xinhua News Agency*, 11 March 2020, http://www.xinhuanet.com/english/2020-03/11/c_138866865.htm

[70] Bao Chuanjian, "China's Virus Fight Squares with Shared Future Concept", *Global Times*, 1 April 2020, https://www.globaltimes.cn/content/1184392.shtml